\*

# DISCOURSE

*Being & Mission*

By

# J.J. BHATT

1

ISBN:

Title:

DISCOURSE:
Being & Mission

Author:

J.J. Bhatt

Published and Distributed by Amazon and Kindle worldwide.

This book is manufactured in the Unites States of America.

# Recent Books by J.J. Bhatt

HUMAN ENDEAVOR: *Essence & Mission,* (2011).

ROLLING SPIRITS: *Being Becoming /*A Trilogy, (2012)

ODYSSEY OF THE DAMNED: *A Revolving Destiny,* (2013).

PARISHRAM: *Journey of the Human Spirits*, (2014).

TRIUMPH OF THE BOLD: *A Poetic Reality*, (2015).

THEATER OF WISDOM, *(2016).*

MAGNIFICENT QUEST: *Life, Death & Eternity,* (2016).

ESSENCE OF INDIA: *A Comprehensive Perspective,* (2016).

ESSENCE OF CHINA: *Challenges & Possibilities*, (2016).

BEING & MORAL PERSUASION: *A Bolt of Inspiration*, (2017).

REFELCTIONS, RECOLLECTIONS & EXPRESSIONS, (2018).

ONE, TWO, THREE... ETERNITY: *A Poetic Odyssey, (*2018).

INDIA: *Journey of Enlightenment,* (2019a).

SPINNING MIND, SPINNING TIME: *C'est la vie*, (2019b).Book 1.

MEDITATION ON HOLY TRINITY, *(2019c), Book 2.*

ENLIGHTENMENT: *Fiat lux,* (2019d), Book 3.

BEING IN THE CONTEXTUAL ORBIT, (2019e).

QUINTESSENCE: *Thought & Action,* (2019f).

THE WILL TO ASCENT: *Power of Boldness & Genius,* (2019g).

RIDE ON A SPINNING WHEEL: *Existence Introspected, (*2020a).

3

# Preface

DISCOURSE: *Being & Meaning* is in pursuit of seeking various possibilities, how to move forward with the constructive dialogues; leading humans to rethink and restart their collective journey toward a world of rhythm, harmony and meaning before the time is up. In particular, it is hope the young minds will consider the matter as presented while searching for their individual path.

J.J. Bhatt

# Contents

# Ascension

Intelligent
Being is the
Real power of
All essences
To be chewed on

When
He evolves so
Does the society
And light is
Everywhere

Also at each
Turning point, he
Defines
The outcome

Intelligent
Awakened being;
Moving
Chaos to order and
Despair to hope

That is when
Human is his own
Beauty and meaning
At the same time...

# Eternal

"I" just an
Ordinary human,
At times, also am
A historic force of
Change too,

If I make-up
My inner mind
To roll the dice on
Time

"I" just an
Ordinary human
Not always so brave

But when
I make up
My freewill, I think
I can climb the steepest
Mount any time

"I" is the
Moral Self who's
Not afraid to probe
Into the realm of my
Own beauty and truth...

# Faith
# Over
# Belief

Faith is
An exclusive power
Emanating from
The solemn soul only

It is independent
Of any belief imposed
By the external
Preaching's, dogmas or
The pseudo-worships

To be specific,
It's the Soul what is
A moral necessity and
Rational intensity to
Open the right trail

Faith
Must be the real
Essence of every inner
Being; guiding toward
The deep meaning of
All that is...

# Noble Mission

Only pure
Humanity shall
Fulfill the ideal
Dreams

So, let us
Learn to walk the
Walk to grasp the
Meaning of our solemn
Journey to the end

No point
In wasting triviality
Of the existence

No point
In fighting for
Different brands of
Geographic gods
When He is the only
ONE

Let us relearn
To move on... for the
Time is slipping away
Quite mercurially by the
Sec...

# The
# Quest

To charter
A path where mind
Begins to understand
The splendor of this
Beautiful existence

To walk
Along a track where
Humanity begins to
Awakened to its common
Sense

That be the
End point and let
It be the journey of
All caring beings

I say,
"Let it be the
Genuine beginning"

Let us walk
Together with great
Lucidity and commitment
And justify our endurance
While here for a brief...

# Mind
# Game

Intelligent being
Waiting to know,
"What is to becoming?"

Being asking,
"What metaphysically
Exists and what is the
Meaning of it all?"

Oh yes,
Intelligent being
Seeking to interpret
The widening experience
Of humanity as such

Meanwhile,
In the great game of
The mind,

There were
The rationalists,
Empiricists and in-between
Them whoever; spinning
Their ideas over and again
And the quest is still on...

# Light & Dark

Great minds
Understood the
Power of
Moral courage and
Rational persuasion,
But the emotive world
Ignored their wisdom,
Alright

Indeed, they were
The truth tellers for
They grasped, "How
To walk along a right
Track..."

Meanwhile,
In this
Super busy world of
Techno-driven
Hedonism

Our struggles
Continues as the
Conscience is leaving
Humanity to be on its
Own...

# Global Choice

The
Noble Soul
Still suspended
Between the
Imperfection and
Perfection

And, the
Transition is the
Biggest challenge,
But not impossible to
Attain

If human is
Ready to fly off the
Imposed beliefs of
Dividing and the
Constant chaos

Time is
Now to rethink
The journey ahead

Time is
Now to be a moral
Courage and to act
Accordingly to fulfill
The waiting mission...

# Mirror

There is
That shining
Mirror
In the dark

In it,
There is the
Image of my Soul
With clarity and
Possibilities for sure

And yet,
I am not awakened
To the task for what
I've been born

What a
Great blunder,
"Am I" in this
Historic set up
To be

Let me
Fight back against
The thick layer of
My ignorance and be
The freewill walking
Along a right trail, again...

# Friendship

Love,
I have never
Left the feelings
That you've been
Questioning lately

Love,
Let's
Just dialogued
With trust and
Sincerity of our
Friendship

Love,
We've to change
Our attitude to keep
The relationship
Strong, as ever

Love,
We're young and
Still long ways to
Go

Dear heart,
Let's make our
Love journey full of
Rhythm, melody and
Meaning...

# Invitation

Life,
At time seems
To be in a state
Of perennial
Chaos

And, we
The ignorant
Beings trying to
Grasp the reality
Through its debris
And dust

Let
Our awakened
Minds put us on
A right path
We've been after
For a long

Come and
Join together and
Be worthy of our births
And be the winners to
The end...

# Be Free

**It's a
Moral necessity
To know
What direction
We've been
Heading**

**For, it's
Paramount to
Know,
If the journey is
All possibilities and
No double-speak at all**

**Time to be
Free from the curse
Of the seven sin**

**Time to be
The thinking being
At this
Critical turning
Point simply...**

# At the Gate

Each
Stands alone
In the final meaning
Of all that is

Each
Must arrive the
Gate of truth on
His/her own while
On the road

Since each
Conscience builds
Mighty humanity,
It's equally
Worthy to pay
Attention to the
Whole

It's the
Holistic world and
Our explorations must
Be a one big team and be
The winners in the game...

# Validation

Light is
Meaningful only
If it prevails good
Over evil

Human is
Worth only
If he's ready to
Be active in making
Of a better world

Talk is
Rewarding if it
Takes toward a
World of hope and
Harmony

Life is
Beautiful only
If every human makes
An effort to keep it
That way...

# Freedom

What
We're
Is a worthy
Issue
To be raised

Where
We're going
Too is a right
Concerned to be
Expressed

Between
Thoughts
And action,
We're the
Freewill and

Once
The choice is
Exercised,
Only consequence
Is the final will and
That's beyond reach...

# Blueprint

Thinkers
Been pursuing to
Know nature of justice,
Virtue, knowledge and
Truth and the quest
Continues even to date

Million
Opinions, views
And perspectives keep
Popping-up time after
Time and the journeys
Still on

That's the
Very dynamics of
Changing nature of
Reality we've been in
For some time

Let everything
Change, but the will
To seek truth must not...

# Reflections

Our many
Possibilities is the
Real strength what
Makes us, "Who
We're at the core"

Our ability
To think creatively
Takes us beyond the
Myopic world

That is the
Genuine essence,
"Who we're and what
We can become"

And, that is the
Where we must
Arrive,
Where we're the
Truth called,
"Peace, harmony and
Hope at all time..."

# Lady
# Love

*L'amoura*
*Toujours,*
Love forever
Is the reality of
Our truth

Don't
Change a bit
Don't run away
From the experience
That we hold heart to
Heart

Oh yes,
My lady of love
Let's just dance and
Be in the state of
Beautiful ecstasy from
Now onward

*L'amoura toujours,*
*L'amoura toujours* so
We shall die together and
Be in eternity forever...

# Measure

Ancient glories
Driven by sacrifices
Either animal or
Human to please
The angry gods

Always
The fear factor
Redressed in the
Name of rituals,
Worships and the
Violent tribal claims

And, madness
Kept moving like
A killer giant wave
Through the sea of
Historic experience

Well, the present
Is no matter than
Before as myopia,
Phobia and insane
Cults; undermining the
Global Spirit of Good...

# The
# Issue

What if
Life
Emerges after
A total death,
Will the seeds of
Evil still grow on
The new scene again!

Will
New religio-lessons
And myths bounce
Back to keep the mind
Under their control

Wonder,
If the seeds of
The seven sin shall
Ever vanish from the
Awakened beings of
Today and tomorrow!

# Let's
# Roll

Let's
Together sail
The mad sea

Let's
Untie ourselves
From the age old
Bloody history of
Our kind

Let's
Come together
To unlock the
Infinite strength
What we've within

Let's
Learn to care
For the Nature
Who's given so much

Let's not
Be greed and selfish
Toward her and of
Course, at each other
I mean, ever again...

# Unknown Trail

Being human
Means a fragile
Experience against
Many odds of life
To be
Walking through

Its fear
Of the unknown
Hanging over his
Head like the
Damocles sword

In his vulnerability,
Myths, beliefs and
Tribal myopia prisoned
Him since the beginning

Well,
As a consequence,
He ended up today;
Living in the world of
Violence's and wars and

The sword is
Still hanging over his
Thick head; perhaps
He doesn't care...

# As Is

Freedom
In reality simply
Extends to the limit
Of our opinions and
In restraining conduct

Beyond the
Perimeter, freedom
Is just a borrowed
Anticipation, greatly
Dependent upon the
Consensus of the whole

Freedom
Often is softened by
The imposed, "Do's
And Don'ts" and there
Is no escape

Freedom
Is well and alive
When a choice is being
Made between thought
And action and then
It's off the control...

# Power
# Within

Only
The enlightened
Understood, "The
Soul is the eternal
Consciousness"

Only
The rational
Mind knew, "The
Meaning of all that is"

Only
Such humans
Can link us to
The holistic reality
We've been in already

There is
No need of Divine
In the set equation
Instead let us
Be aware of the
Power of the moral
Spirit and

Let's be
At the steering wheel
And keep sailing all the
Way to the waiting truth...

# Lux

Light
Is the eternal will
Guiding to the right
Direction

Light
Is the brilliance
Of the human essence
At the core already

Why then
Be afraid walking
Through the dark
Tunnel of anxiety and
Despair

Keep trusting
The moral self and
Continue the journey
Yes,
Even through the
Stygian nights after
Nights;

Still you'll
Succeed in the end
For the light within
Must be the real guide.

# Grand Matrix

What we
Understand is the
Consequence of our
"Intuitive assumptions"
May be

Perhaps,
Only the rational
Mind would be the
Best reader of truth
We've been after

But then
We're spinning
Within the
Grand matrix of
Conceptuality

That is
Why "Perfection"
Seems a far cry from
What the total reality
Must be...

# Being &
# Essence

We humans
Indeed are the
Cosmic seeds

Albeit sparks
Of intellectual
Mysticism to know
The meaning of us
In this vast unknown
Called, "All that is"

Our journey
Is to transform the
Self from ignorance
To the enlighten and

Be in-charge of the
Common destiny called,
"Harmony, Hope and
Peace."

# My
# Song

Oh
Charming lady
Of my dream,
How long
Will you tease
My waiting heart

Don't you
See times slipping
Away so quick

Don't you
See feelings
Been waiting
For sometime

Drop the
Façade and come
And dance with me
All the way to the
Never-ending love,
Yes, to never ending
Love...and love, only...

# Restortion

In nutshell,
What we are
Here is to
Experience our
Individual moral
Self

That is
The first step,
Albeit the first
Principle to jump
Start the journey
Ahead

Let us
Endeavor to
Reach
The set mission
And be
Worthy spirits
Of all time

Let us
Free ourselves
From falsity, pseudo-
Beliefs and the
Insane claims;
Justifying violence's
And repeated
Blood spills...

# Recurrences

We're
Genuine
Participants
In the finite universe
That we know bit
Better than yesterday

We're
The aware souls
Knowing well,
"We're spinning
Into
The endless cycle
Of birth, death and
Rebirth"

In other words,
All remains the
Same and each
Enters the world

At every
Turning; returning
To the same beginning
Again and again...

# Destiny

When shall
We learn to reason
And fight against
The built-in ignorance
And be free humans

When shall
Be bold to take a
Stand against those
With arrogance and
Indifferent attitude;
Obstructing the progress

When shall
We wake-up and know,
"Each is responsible of
His/her conduct in
Strengthening the moral
Inspiration of the whole..."

# Blind Alley

Why argue and
Fight out of sheer
Ignorance,
When
Life can be made
More meaningful
And full of joy

Why fire
Big guns and send
Robo killers when
Deaths and destructions
Are the consequence

Why preach
Mercy, love and care
When they do just
The opposites to their
Fellow humans

So long,
Humans are not
Morally decent and
Driven by ignorance,
Deaths and destructions
Shall be the constant
Consequence....

# Wave
# Makers

We're
The nanosec sparks
Born to cool off the
Fiery universe

For
Each is a
Mind everywhere
Looking for meaning
Of all that is

We're
The certainty caught
Into the reality of
Uncertainty whence our
Struggles and chaos

The challenge,
"What is our role
In the larger whole and
How to be free ourselves
From the seven sin"

# Big
# Grasp

Did we
Ever realize
There is no
Perfection in the
Big picture of
All there is

That means,
The First Cause
Whatever it may be
Is not either

That
Necessitates
Every being
To go from
Imperfection to
Perfection on their
Own, but the
Journey is
Never, so smooth...

# Open
# Window

From
Consistency of
Laws of nature,
There emerges
The rational insight
Depicting beauty of the
Holistic connection
Alright

It is
The creative
Curiosity and
Predilection to grasp
The truth after all is
The force behind

Yes,
From consistency
Of the inner being,
" I and the infinite
Possibilities,
We're dancing
In the cosmic charm
Called, *Unity* alright..."

# Big Spin

Perhaps
We're the genuine
Players in this finite
Reality where we
Belong

Yes,
We're indeed
The determined
Pursuers of "What Is"
In this otherwise
Aimlessly expanding
Universe

We keep
Spinning
Our thoughts,
Ideas and endeavors
Over and again in this
Beauty of all that is and
No full answers in return,
Thus far...

# Return

Moral being
Is the final frontier
Of his conscience for
That shall lead him to
The path of
Enlightenment
In the end

Meanwhile
Time is now
To rethink and reform
The old habits and to
Chart a new journey
Once again

Time to
Rid off the
Divisional mentality,
Fanaticism and
Excessive hedonism

And let's
Fall back to the
Simplicity, unity and
The feelings of humanity
And be the genuine
Humans we're once...

# Journey

Being
Becoming
Is our reality alright
And no point standing
Still and keep
Complaining out of
Ignorance

The issue,
Do we've a
Courage to evolve
From Perceptuality
To spirituality and
Be the masters of our
Collective destiny

After all
We're the ever
Widening circles of
Consciousness and

Its time
To reckon our truth
And begin the walk
Toward the final goal
With all
The full-confidence...

# Written

Don't
Run away from
The charming feelings
You've been holding
So long

Don't
Avoid expressing
Your feelings toward
This guy

Yes, I'm
Serious for the
Souls have already
Understood

The meaning of
You and I
When we first said,
"Hello with a warm
Smiles"

Well here
We're sweetheart
Waiting to begin a
New journey together
All we need is,
"You to wake-up to
The reality we're in..."

# Illuminators

Let "I"
Mean
An inspiration
Of the whole and not
An individual itself

Let "I"
Point upward
And be the glowing
Spiritual spark ever

Let "I"
Experience Truth
In time to know the
Essence of all that is
Around

Let "I"
Be the freewill and
Moral good to build
A better world

Let "I"
Be the inclusiveness
In its all respect and
Be a genuine human
Being at last...

# Twin
# Reality

In the
Dominion of
Abstraction being
Alone is the maker
Of his reality

That reality
Is but the reflection
Called, "Thought &
Action"

In the
Dominion of
Empirical subjectivity
Only to be befuddled
And be despaired

Two modes
Of reality:
The former
Where freewill is
Sovereign and the latter
Where human is merely
A borrowed time only...

# Beginning

While gazing
The cosmic beauty
For the first time,
The curious human
Must have wondered,
"What is it all about?"

He then
Suddenly reckoned,
"To seek a deep
Understanding must
Be the reason he
Has arrived
On the scene"

Intelligent
Human since then
Kept probing, "Who
He is and what is the
Direction to untie the
Riddles before passing
On to eternity..."

# Caveat

Being
Today seems
Slowly sinking into
The sea of the
Techno addiction and
There is no concern

It's the sweet
Comforts to live
A hedonistic life and
All the speedy work
That it brings with a
Single click

Soon,
Folks will be
Honored to be
The consumers only
As monthly check will
Be paid automatically

Of course,
Nothing is a free
Lunch and the price;
Letting the smart
Thinking machines to
Be the masters thus loss
Of humanity in return
Only!

# Rebirth

At
Prodigious
Depth,
Every being is a
Kernel of goodwill
And hope essentially

That is
The core of his
Very essence to be
Remembered daily

Being is
Free only if he is
Aware of his own
Genuine identity

Let him
Know, "He alone
Is the eternal
Possibility"

Let him
Lift the
Humanity with the
Same awakened
Spirit..."

# Old
# Buddies

It was
A beautiful event
At the yearly
Celebration
Of the old friends

Yes, it was
A great time to
Reminiscent all the
Great adventures of
Our youthful times

The crazy
Bike rides, the
Risky canoeing in
The great Colorado
And the hiking to
The Mount McKinley

What a grand
Journey together
As buddies forever
What a
Beautiful memories
Meant forever...

# Magic
# As Is

Don't say,
It's all over for
Love never quits
The experience

Don't say,
We're not for
One another for
Memories sing
Otherwise

Come
Back to me for
I shall be waiting
Always for you

Yes,
Come back to
The love that still
You've in your heart

Every time
I see you, I see
The tears of your
Soul and I know you've
Never gone that far

Come back and be
The happiness
That we were since
We took the vows...

# Our Time

Emergence
Of an illumined
Mind is a moral
Necessity in our
Time

For humanity
Is in suspension
Between good and
Evil habits and

The consequences are
Nothing but war and
Peace, right and wrong
Love and hate and
Many mores

Sadly,
The negativity is
Surpassing in our
Time as irrational
Actions are governing
The fate of our freedom,
Peace and compassion...

# Heroic
# March

Who we're
And what we ought
To be shall define
Our common destiny
In the end

Let the
Journey be directed
Toward Good of the
Whole

Let the
Common-sense
Go into effect to be
Off the cage of never
Ending rage, blood spills
And the insane wars

Let us
Gear up to be the
Heroes of our time and
Redefine the journey
We've been on...

# Caveat Emptor

When
We're the
Spiritual beings

Why
Get so much
Tangled

Into the
Material world
Driven

By the
Over consumption,
Junk eatery and be
Fat and sick

While clever
Pharma and
Big boys stay healthy
And super rich

Think and
Think again and
Be smart not to be
Sucked into their
Luring vortex, please...

# Know
# Thy Truth

Human
Mind is always
Studded with the
Jewels of metaphysics,
Ethics, aesthetics and
So on

Each offering
A given dimension
To understand the
World and the self,
Per se

That is
The epicenter of
Every being what
We call, "Noble Soul"

The soul
That is the real
Participant in the
Eternal cosmic game
While the corpse is no
More

Please honor
The wishes of the
Noble Soul and be
Grateful of having
Such an enlightened
Spirit within...

# Being &
# Morality

Moral
Means to be
The disciplined
Mind

Moral
Makes human
To behave well

Moral
Means to be
Well matured
Being

Moral
Means to have
A strong will

Moral
Is the passage
To the state of
Enlightenment

Moral
Means to be
Independent of any
Imposed belief by others...

# Life As Is

Life
Is all we've
To fulfill our
Dreams

Life
Is to reach
The set goals

Life is
Where we meet
A soul who's
Ready to be the best
Trust, it's called,
"Love"

From love,
We bring the
Off-springs and

Tell 'em to be
Heroes not for their
Greed, but the good
Of the whole

That is
Meaning of life and
That life we must learn
To shape it well

From the
Beginning for the
Time is brief indeed...

# Magic
# Mind

**Mind**
**Being ornamented**
**With the issues of**
**Metaphysics, ethics,**
**Aesthetics and much**
**More**

**So it's been**
**On fire to know**
**The answers to**
**All his queries and**
**The great riddle**
**Continues to date**

**Well,**
**That's the**
**Very epicenter of**
**His "Intellectual**
**Mysticism" and the**
**Journey rolls on**

**Mind**
**What a wonderful**
**Gift of reason and**
**Moral freewill, yet**
**To be exercised more...**

# Infatuation

You
May not
Be aware dear
Sweetheart

But
I am always
In love with you
Yes in my
Thoughts and
Dreams

When
We pass each
Other through
Narrow corridor
At the school

For heaven
Sake, "Why don't
You care to give a
Smile at least?"

Why can't
You take the
First bold step;
Least say,
"Hello to my waiting
Heart, please!"

# Will
# To be

Intelligent
Being an eternal
Thought into the
Magnificent reality
He's been wrapped
Around

It's an
Ever expanding
Sphere of all his
Struggles to know
The truth

He's ready
To embattle the
Ignorance and be
The winner in this
Enigmatic game

Let him
Spark and vanish
The dark life
After life and

Let his
World be the total
Truth and nothing but
The Truth to the end...

# Evanesce

Dear Heart,
We're not the
Same
What we're

And,
We're in the
Struggle to be
One once again

Life
Brings streams
Of turning point
And there ain't
An escape

Time to
Deal
With reality
As is and

Keep the
Fire going
With compassion,
Understanding and
Good old friendship...

# Passengers

Death
Is just another
New beginning

It's an
Adventure beyond
And nothing to be
Feared

Life
That we lived is
One of the chapters
And many more yet
To go

In this
World it was all
About good and evil,
Right and wrong and
So on

Over there,
There is simplicity,
Love and harmony
With the totality of
All That Is...

# Rational
# Spirit

The measure
Is the degree of
Awareness

What is meant
To be the rational
Insight

Indeed,
It is all about
Self-awareness of
The mind

A mind of
The universe driven
By the power of moral
Goodwill

Let human
Endeavor be to
Conquor the mind
And

Ride toward
The ultimate truth,
"Who we're and
What we can become..."

# Aim

We're the
Flow of events
Indeed, we're the
Wave-makers and
We're the architects
Of our beliefs and
Dreams as well

Of course,
We're the sole
Seeds of good and evil
And the judges of our
Historic experience

Against such
A reality, we must be
Shaped by the self-
Inspection independent
Of any imposed will

That is
The path we must
Be chugging along
Without fear, but with
Calm and moral courage...

# We the People

Human
Existence is basically
Relationship, understanding
And the desire to roll along
The same destiny

After all,
All that exists is
Ephemeral ideas, fleeting
Memories and the recurrences
Of joy and grief

While walking
Along such a narrow
Trail of many unknowns,
Folks need others to give
Hope, love and courage
To make it through

That is
Where the essence
Of humanity emerges
On the scene and
That is where reckoning
Must flash,

"We're the
Contextual beings and
We need a Global harmony
To survive and succeed
Not today but tomorrow
As well..."

# H-Equation

While
Scanning the
Game of existence,
I realize the human
Equation seems
Quite wobbly

Each is
Born with equal
Love and care, but
The later years don't
Remain the same

Ideally,
Each is the
Humanity of good
And each is a
Truth of humanity
At the core

In reality,
Sadly each is not
Yet there and the
Equation needs to be
Refined and to be
Completed in time...

# Courage,
# We Must

No point
Tolerating the
Realm where human
Freedom is limited

We know
Well, reason and
Moral good are the
Evil busters and

Why then
We sit ideal
And wait for others
To go into action

No point
Living where
Human spirit is
Waning and let the
Tears follow the trend

Time to
Roll-up the sleeves
And get ready with
New vigor to change
The world for good...

# Sanity
# In Order

Let's learn to
Dissolve all differences
And come to our senses
And begin the walk along
The new path of being
The awakened spirits

That is
How we shall endure
Through the evil forces
Of our time and that is
The legacy we must pass
On

Let the
Young also know,
"Societal responsibility
Is more urgent than
Demanding individual
Rights and freedom"

Time to
Bring some
Sanity when there
Is an unbridle
Killer blending:
Hatred, violence's and
The gun culture...

# New Path

All the
Trials and Errors
Of the journey
May take sometime
To be transformed
Into one cohesive
Triumph

Introspection
Always be the
First principle to
Begin the task
Ahead

That is
The way to
Reform human
Nature at the
Core

Let
The ageless
Trials and Errors
Of yesterday turn
Into one collective
Destiny of good...

# Arrival

Let's not
Forget, " the
Arrival of human
That brought the
Creative boldness
To clarify all that
Is still in flux"

Of course,
Humans are
The expression of
Spiritual power
Within

They are
Indeed the
Brave explorers of
All that is

Let them
Glorify
Their births

Let them
Triumph over
Own nemesis within
And be free forever...

# Clarity

God,
Cannot be branded,
Codified or be abused
For pseudo-claims

No single
Sect got monopoly
In His Name

For He belongs
Not just the tiny
Myopic humans, but to
Mega-Universe itself

Time to
Reset the sanity
In order and begin
To know, "God is
In our Global act of
Harmony, peace
And hope"

Let it be
Our new wisdom,
Albeit a common sense
In action and let us
Learn to be free again...

# Being & Truth

In this
Brilliance of the
Magnifique reality

Suddenly,
There is a spark
Flashing through
The dark and

I the
Truth stands
Before with a
Smile and declares,

"A being
Who is an
Individual of rational
Nature shall always
Move forward"

"But how is it
So?"I asked with
Some intrigue

"For he is a
Moral Goodwill, but
His action is a necessity."

# Unsettled

Why this
Subjective mind
Keeps drowning into
Contradictions,
Confusions and the
Stubborn chaos

Sadly,
Great ideas
Keep floating
Aimlessly at times
And human is
Alienated
In the process

In such a
State of mind,
There is the
Locked-in struggle of
"Hit and miss"
And not much gets
Accomplished

Subjective being
Still on the highway
Of his "Objective truth,"
But the journey never ends...

# Petite Souls

Children
So happily learning
New lessons at the
School

Children
Getting the first
Experience how
To be civil in
Life

Children
There they
Begin the journey
To be good human
Beings

That is
The Temple of
Their truth where
They become aware
Of their world

And,
Suddenly they
Become victims
Of an insane mind;
Destroying their
Innocent dreams, so
Untimely right on
The spot...

# The Trail

Let I
Walk along the
Trail where clarity
Is the light

Let I
Wait a while
Before launching
My ambition right
Away

I know
The trail is quite
Winding and there're
No signs to show the
Right direction

In such
A blind journey
Of my reality,
Mustn't I be guided
By the Moral Self
And the rational
Perspective that I
Still hold!

# Illumination

Being
What a unique
Mirror where the
World sees in, his
Ideas, dreams and
Goodwill

Being
Always a sum
Total of cognitive
And emotive
Universe

Being
Never hiding
From his projected
Image to the world

Being,
The strong thread
Treading through
Complexity and chaos

Yet, capable of
Winning the game
To the end, if he wakes
Up to the build-in inner
Strength...

# Being &
# Essence

Existence
Necessities essence
To know
The self identity

Indeed,
To begin the journey
Toward the Unknown

Existence
Must have its moral
Content and a rational
Goal to lead a purpose-
Driven life

Existence
Never be painted
With despair, alienation
Or the defeatist attitude

For humanity
Depends on the enlightened
Minds that can bring hope,
Harmony and the meaning
To the troubled world...

# Pragmatic

Morality
Though deep desire
Of many, only the
Few are blessed to
Exercise it

Beyond,
Reality is mainly
Greed driven and
Always a silent
Disturbance to the
Mind

Human
Mind that is why
Be disciplined
With reason and
Compassion at
An early age

For everything
Pops-up first in the
Mind and whatever
Consequences thereof
To the world either
Good or otherwise...

# Great
# Glow

We humans
Simply flow with
The magnificent Glow
Of the dynamic universe
Every moment of our
Finite reality

The great Glow
Appears and disappears
From our consciousness
Time and time again;
Triggering the birth-death
Cycle over and again

That is
The holistic reality
We live in and there
Is no pure freedom, but
To flow with the Great
Glow all through,
Eternity...

# Need
# To Talk

Saints, thinkers
And ordinary folks
Warned us,
"Human is diseased
By the seven sin"

The message
Always felt on
Deaf ears for historic
Experience is the
*Prima facies*

They
Asked to believe
In God, myth or
Whatever helped
To be wiser than
Before and yet our
Human nature hasn't
Changed

Seems
Our collective
Journey got to go
Long ways before
We are free from the
Individual enemy
Within...

# An
# Insight

When
The world is
Caught into the
Whirlwinds of
Destruction and
Death

Let us
Come to our
Common sense and
Lifting humanity
To the apotheosis of
Required ethics

Only
Moral sanity and
Rational intentions
Shall bring in
Harmony and
Peace

That is
The only practical
Endeavor and that is
The only choice
To reach the ultimate
Mission we've been
Born for...

# Conscious Being

How dare
We forget the
Simple truth,
"The soul is the
Only
Eternal strength
In this otherwise
Corrupted reality"

That is
What we know
So well, but refuse
To admit it whence
The struggles on

To keep
The individual
Soul healthy and
Happy
There is a
Work to be done

Let it
Spark with harmony,
Moral rhythm and
Rational intentionality,
I mean
While walking along the
Track...

# Gauntlet

Let be
Declared boldly
To the world,
"Human is the
Slave of the seven
Sin"

That is
The bill board needs
To be hanged on every
Thick head

Yet, human
Alone is supreme
To be the illuminating
Winner in the great
Game

Only if
He wakes-up
The potentiality and
Dares to reach out to
His beauty and truth...

# Early
# Dawn

I am unity
Of all the totality
That is my thinking,
Passion and curiosity

Yes, I am
The traveler
Simply passing
Through my given
Time and

I am
Untouched either
By joy or grief, but
Staying on the
Right track

Yes, my
Time is brief and
The trail too long

And I've
My primary
Mission to attain
As soon that I must...

# Miracle

Meditation
Is a mystical
Experience
Every time

It enables
I to clarify the
Sticking issues and
Frees me from the
Million worries

Mediation
Always purifying
My thoughts, words
And deeds

Meditation
Strengthening my
Inner will to climb
Any steep mount I
Dare to take on

Meditation
Takes many years
To mature
After all its not a
Magic wand but a
Disciplining, the mind...

# Being & Existence

In the
Silence of the
Night
As I stare
At the cosmic
Bright

I reckon,
"I is th spirit,
Albeit a tiny spark
In an ever expanding
Possibilities"

That is
Where I begin
To know my
"Mystical identity"

I, a definite
Link with all
That I see, think
And willing to go
Beyond my death

Yes,
To grasp, "What is
It all about" with
No further question
To be raised...

# Come & Dance

Hey, hey
My sweet gal
Haven't we talked
Enough,
I mean
Haven't debated
Enough

Come,
Let's dance with
World of our silent
Love and be merry
Forever

Hey, hey
My dear gal,
Why just stand still
And avoid the romance
While the times slipping
Away from our hearts

Come,
Let's climb the
Highest dream of
Our life to be happy
Over and again that
Is what I mean it,
"Our love forever..."

# Long
# Journey

History
Is defined by the
Good and evil nature
Of humans mainly

Shining
Civilizations
Bloomed cause of
The Good while the
Bloody wars were
The evil forces of the
Corrupted minds
As well

That is the
Silently oscillating
Mind; depicting its
Regular ebbs and
Flows ...sometimes
So bright and
Sometimes just not

Time to swim
Out of the wild sea and
Be on the *terra firma*

And share
A meaningful life with
All others to the end...

# Be the
# Hero

Life is an
Open book waiting
To be filled with good
Thoughts and deeds

That is how
A being communes
With the reality; near
And beyond

Let each
Amplify personhood
To change the world
With a begnin aim

Let each
Be the hero of
The story called,
"His open journey,
Indeed..."

# Inner
# Being

What if
Being is in
Essence, "Morality
Objectified"

Will that
Set his journey
In the right direction
Alright or what

After all
Life is constantly
Swirled by the myriad
Uncertainties and
Anxiety is on the rise

In such a
State of
Unpredictability,
What else but to
Rely upon his inner
Being; what is a
Moral self only!

# Endurance

We young
Friends took off
Bike rides all the
Way to the mount
Inspiration

Our collective
Alacrity put us
Half way
To the peak
With much ease

But in the
Upper half of the
Climb, we were
Separated spirits,
It seemed

Most couldn't
Make it and few
Still kept pushing
With their inner
Strengths

At the
Top only one of
Us conquered the
Challenge and we
Saluted her as our
New hero at once ...

# Renewal

Do we,
Ever care to know,
"We humans got the
Power to draw out
Meaning from a
Constant chaos"

Do we,
Ever care to know,
"History is a warning
Asking to avoid all
Blunders and sins of
The past"

Why
Do we fail to
Understand the
Unintended consequences
Of our asinne adventures:
Vanity, envy and greed

Why can't
Be smart enough
To push for goodness,
Tolerance and stand
For peace and peace alone
For a change...

# Metamorphosis

The will
To evolve is a
Survival instinct and
Not a divinely notion,
At least in certain sense
Of the reality we're in

Each being
What a fractional
Spark rolling toward
His set destiny alright

Each an
Ever changing shape
And form from dark
To the light indeed

Each
Constantly drawn
Toward his own
Being Becoming and
Each is the turning
Point while the spark
Is on...

# Great Walk

Our
Birth defines
The base reference
And where the inner
Light begins to get
Brighter with time,

Only if the road is
Clear and no detours
On the way

That is the
Way to our big
Dream and

That is the
Celebration of
Our noble mission
To the top

Make the
Right choice where
Freewill is your best
Pal and walk the walk
All the way to the truth
That you've been waiting
For a long...

# Off the Cage

Its
The human
Who's the
Complex of all
That we think it is

Where falsity,
Religio-dogmas
And treating others
Outside being
"Enemies" is the
Insanity per se

That is
Where we witness
The complete failure
Of humanity and

That is
Where we must
Awaken the collective
Responsibility and
Erase old blunders and
Their killing instinct...

# We

Of course,
Time is here now
To change the
Common way of
Living with greed
And vanity

Time to
Look beyond to
Guard the future
Of our kids

Time to
Drop the old habits
Of violence and the
Constant blood spill

Time to
Wake up to the
Reality we're facing
Today

Time to
Save humanity and
The Planet itself from
Ourselves...

# Progress
# Report

The notion
Peace has no
Meaning
When human is
Under the spell of
The seven sin

The idea
Perfect society
Remains a dream
When human nature
Hasn't changed a bit

Future
Can't be assured
For our kids,
If we refuse to leave
The rusted cage

That is
The synopsis of
The twenty-first
Century human
Progress and
Still moving at
A snail speed in this
Speedy digital age!

# Dear Maya

A word
About Dear,
"Maya"
She's
Interplay
Between the finite
And the infinite;
Sort of "Hide &
Seek" game

There is
The thin veil
Called, "Teasing
Truth" keeps on
Guessing at all the
Time

In such
A wondering
Milieu, the finite
Is determined to
Pierce through the
Veil

But three
Wild dogs: Vanity,
Greed and Solipsism
Won't permit the passage
Through...

# Reckoning

To be
The subject of
An enlightened
World

Each has to
Be aware of the
Self and the reality
Around

To be
The human of
Meaning,
Let moral self
Dictate the course
At every turn

In other
Words, to build
A better humanity,
Each has to take
Responsibility first

Damn right,
Let's get off the
Shadows and be the
Light to reach the
Perfection of our collective
Dream at the same time...

# Be
# Bold

Let's
Affirm,
"We're the reality
Of our
Individual will"

Yes,
We're the
Sum total of
All the dreams we
Hold

We're
The human
In quest of our
Own collective
Divinity and be
Free

Let it
Be our collective
Determination
To know the waited
Truth on our own

Let's learn
To be brave and
Dare to think outside
The age old cage...

# Hey Love

Hey lovely
Gal how long
You're gonna make
I wait

Hey gal,
Listen what I've
To say,
"Our loves
Been ready to
Smile again"

Why run
Away from this
Beauty called,
"Love"

Why can't
You face the
Real feelings of
Your heart

Hey sweet
Gal be a courage
And be mine for
We've loved many
Times before..."

# Sanguine

No point
In let the time
Slip away for
Nothing

No point
In complaining
Forever and doing
Nothing in return

Yes, life
Has a meaning
Yes, it has a
Goal to be
Achieved

Just get off
Your pessimism,
May be nihilistic
Attitude and roll
The self along the
Inspiring track
Again

Let the
Indefatigable will
Be your power to
Ride you through
The optimism; taking
You to the real truth...

# Be
# Delighted

Let's
All relearn
To value our
Collective journey
With tolerance,
Understanding and
Moral point of view

That's
Not a utopian
Whim, but the
Pragmatic strategy
To define a better
Future for the kids

Let's not
Destroy whats
Good in us, but let's
Not hesitate to erase
Whats not

Let's
Think above and
Beyond our turmoil
Times...

# The
# Force

Once again,
It's a reminder,
"I" is the essence
Of  everything
That defines the
Total-experience

"I" stands
For the inner
Freedom to direct
The right trail and
Be worthy of my
Own being

Let "I"
Never be a slave
To falsity, bigotry
And hypocrisy

Let "I"
Be the force of
History to bring
Rhythm, melody and
Meaning...

# Aim High

Being
Is the cosmic gift
To bring in beauty
And truth

Indeed,
He's the awakened
Soul to know the
Meaning on his own

He is
The possibility
To experience peace
And harmony for a
Very long

That is
How we shall
Redeem, our
Imperfection to
Receive perfection
In return

All that would
Be of course, defined
By our endeavors and
Open-minds; taking us
From despair to hope and
From the darkness
To the light...

# Upwells

Morality
Must be upwelling
Waves from the
Inner spirit to
Sustain the world
Of dignity to all

Rational
Vigor too
What a powerful
Surge
From the awakened
Soul simply;

Asking
To know the
Enigmatic reality
With full clarity

"All that is"
Seems one big puzzle
To reset right
Understanding called,
"Truth "and

The truth
Is nothing, but
The resolution of
What is naturally
Noble and good...

# Twist of Fate

Being
Alone is historic
Force that's willing
To define the essence,
"Why existence has
Validity, possibility and
Be an enlightened spirit"

Everything
There is,
Is the consequence
Of his thoughts, words
And deeds, but it's just
A finite point of view

Well it's an
Imminent twist
Of fate, his story
Still remains unfinished
For not knowing the world
That's far and beyond...

# In
# Action

A well
Organized
March called,
"Save Humanity"
Walked with courage
And million signs to
Awaken
The slumbering
Fellow humans

"Stop the
Society falling into
The hands of the
Greed at the top"

"Stop the
Evil forces controlling
The tender minds"

"Stop the
Slavery in-progress
Through the smart
Machines"

"Stop the
Insanity of fake
News, violence's
And the bloody wars..."

# Voice

"Dad and mom,
Why do you fight like
Two enemies?"

Parents were
Stupefied by
What they heard.

"If you keep on
Battling daily, why did
You bring us in the world?"
Kids in unison demanded.

"See children, our human
Nature is not perfect and so
Is the relationship," dad
Tried to explain.

"Yes children, your dad
Is right for a change," mom
Said it with a touch of satire

"Well what about our
Feelings, our love...our
Dreams to be somebody?"

"We're sorry, if we hurt
You two" parents confessed.

"Just stop fighting and please
Be good human beings and
Help us to be good in return"

# Aesthetica

Seems
Art is the only
Creative consciousness
That can transcend the
World beyond

It can also
Seize the best spark
Of any romance either
Here or wherever else

Being and art,
The tandem is the
Best meaning that
Can commune with
The whole Universe

Only the
Creative minds
Know their individual
Moral Self and the
Colorful beauty and
Truth of the reality,
They're in...

# Forever

What a
Charming feelings
To have met you for
The first time

What a
Sparkling smile
What a
Beauty of your
Big heart and the
Unforgettable friendly
Stare
Still I remember
So well

After many
Decades of our joint
Journey, I still recall
That first meeting quite
Well

I may
Say with a petite
Brag, "We're young
And good-looking;

Carrying
Lot of dreams with our
Lovely feelings and that
We know, silently so well..."

# The
# Stroll

**As we**
**Keep walking**
**Along the life of**
**Our given time**

**We**
**Constantly**
**Create our reality,**
**Indeed**

**Yes, we**
**Keep flowing**
**Along the trail**

**A trail of**
**Our wishes, goals**
**And in knowing,**
**"What is it all about?"**

**That is**
**The endeavor**
**That is**
**The existential**
**Pleasure and**

**That is**
**The magic of**
**Creative being in**
**Action...**

# Contemplation

What is
Missing from the
Perfection to be

What is
The reason
We exists in this
Troubled world

What if
Such queries be
Answered with the
Moral dimension or
What?

How do we
Go beyond the
World of despair
And death and be
The awakened being

How do
We relearn to be
The simple humans
We were once and

To  lift
Humanity with such
A rational goodwill for
A change!

# Great
# Spin

If
"All that is"
What is perceived
And willing to be
Nothingness

Will it
Distort our dreams,
Our goals or the
Pursuit to know the
Truth

How
Can we be sure
In the reality where
Uncertainty rules

How
Do we go beyond
With such a serious
Assumption, I mean
With what hope...

# Twists & Turns

Being
Into the world of
Subjectivity

How do we
Balance between,
"What is good and
What is not?"

And how do
We render
A good judgment
To the war that is
Just or may not

Morality,
Again a contentious
Challenge and
How do we
Exercise it when
Euthanasia is the
Challenge

Life
Always a stubborn
Big test while trying
Toward the goal of
Perfection...

# Being & Relativity

When
Night is silent
And there is the
Drizzling sound of
Nature

I keep thinking,
"How to assess
Life that I am here
For a brief"

I mean,
"Where do I
Stand in this reality
Of growth and change"

Again,
On one hand,
I think I am the
Meaning in this
Grand matrix and

On the
Other, sometimes
I feel am the
Hedonistic pig that's
Living off for nothing...

# A Point

All is Simply
A conceptual
Point of view only
And shall not reach
The set truth ever

It's the
Make belief castle
Of inclusions and
Exclusions and we
Call it, "What a
Wonderful world"

Not surprisingly,
It's the civilized being
Who is the real culprit
In the game

Indeed unleashing
Evil forces for a
Long whence the
State we are living
It through today

That is our
Collective truth
And that is where
We must begin to
Rethink and make
Our smart moves...

# Our
# Time

Modern
Humans caught
By the milieu of
Insecurity and
The uncertainty,
Alright

And guardians
Not paying enough
Attention how to
Find the right path

All reality
Seems fear and anxiety
Of the survival of life
And the Planet itself

Modern
Humans caught by
The asinne violence's,
Destructions and deaths
And still the guardians
Are sleeping at the wheel...

# On
# The Road

Always
Wondered the
Challenge of
Metaphysical
Equilibrium in the
World that is in
An eternal turmoil

And why this
Struggle and fear
When there is so much
Beauty and truth to be
Inspired

Why we
The intelligent beings
Are denied by the pious
Servants not to query
Beyond

Let
The moral will and
The power of reason
Free us and
Show us the real path
That is ahead...

# Illumined

Being is
Born to hold order
And ensure harmony
As the final goal

Indeed,
Let his moral
Goodness triumph
To the end

Being is
Born to secure
Clarity over confusion
And bring reason to
Save his noble soul

Yes,
From the constant
Bickering, despair
And insane claims...

# Players &
# Trainers

We're
Clowns doing our
Circus acts day in
And day out and
Hardly anyone cares

We keep
Juggling chaos
And order at every
Minute and there are
No spectators to applaud
Our magic plays

We keep
Training
All wild animals
For the great thrills
Of children and adults

Well,
In the process,
We forget to
Train ourselves,
"How to
Cooperate to give
Happiness to others!"

# Our
# Story

Once Nature
Was worshipped
In the name of
Earth, water, wind,
Fire and the Sun
And there was
Tranquility in the
Minds of the ancients

Later
Evolved myths
And organized
Beliefs and the world
Underwent a good share
Of its blunders and
Blood spills

Well, the deep
Wounds from the
Past haven't healed
Yet and the madness
Keeps dancing with
Greater intensity ever

Meanwhile,
Individual moral Self
Is caught into the
Killer storm called,
"Insanity." What a pity!

# Rudderless

Why
Go so long on
A voyage where
There's darkness and
The formless void,
Named, "Nothingness"

Why
Try to beat the
Mighty Blue Sea when
The ship is rudderless

Why did
We evolve toward
Such an
Endless adventure

Will there
Be a sudden
Change of wind
To lift us

From
Meaningless to the
Highest point of a
Meaningful
Human or what?

# Noble Warriors

Never
Undermine our
Courage and self-
Confidence

For each
A master piece,
*Magnum opus* of
His/her grand story
To be left behind

For each
Is an immense
Power of creativity
And reason to shook- up
The evil from within

Each is a
Shield to save the
Noble soul from the
Seven sin and

Each is a
Warrior born to
Conquor the mind,
In essence, only...

# Rolling
# Spirits

As we
Keep walking
Through the storm
Of life and time

We often are
Torn between the
Reality of unity and
Dividing mentality

In unity,
We are reason,
Courage and creators
Of new future of harmony
And hope

In dividing mentality,
We are victims of
Chaos, lies and betrayals
Of our individual being

In unity,
We're the
Divine Spirits and
"Being Becoming"

In dividing mentality,
We're the nemesis to
One another and existence
Has no meaning but the
State of sheer ignorance...

# We
# Exists

There is a
New song being
Ringing into the
Hearts of those
Willing to explore
Their individual truth:

We're the
Imperishable souls
Keep dancing into
This holistic reality
And we never stop
To enjoy what is given
To us

We're the
Daring ones ready
To take on any
Challenge that's in our
Way

We're also
The magicians playing
Out our creative whims
And willing to reset new
Trails to the waiting truth...

# Winners

Monumental
Grandeur is only
For the heroes who
Leave a great legacy
Behind

Oh yes,
There were once
Many kings and
Great warriors,

But if they left
Deep wounds and
Deaths; they were
Good only for a brief

And those
Others who left
Moral inspiration and
Courage to lift the
Spirit of humanity is
Remembered forever...

# Stay
# Focus

What may
Come
Let's move on
With the question
We hold at this very
Time

No point in
Going around in
Circle and let the
Moments fly away
For nothing

Only way
To know the nature
Of totality of experience
Is to keep rolling forward
With a single intention
Only

Just keep
Going toward the
Brilliance of the mind
And seek beauty and
Truth within...

# The Stream

It was
A Moonlit night
And all was so
Tranquil and
The stream kept
Flowing toward its
Set destination

Suddenly,
There emerged
Bunch of folks from
Beneath the surface
Of the stream

They waived
Hello and kept
Enjoying the swim

"Who are you folks?"

"We're you and you
Shouldn't be surprised"

I was jolted with their
Response

"Don't worry
You shall appear
And disappear in the
Rolling stream just
Like we do"
They took a dive and
Were no more on the scene...

# Ever
# Lasting

When
The soul is freed
From the turmoil's of
The mind

At that point,
Burial or cremation
Two different ways;
Ending up the same

That is
The real unity of
The Universe, at last
That is
The new journey
Of those who're no
More

There is
No need for a
Closure for them
There is
No need to drop
Tears in their
Names

They're
Happily their way
To eternity for a
Deeper meaning
While being here...

# Patterns

Once
They turned the
Captured soldiers
Into slaves

Still they do it
In a different ways,
But with a same old
Intention too

Slavery
Always a stigma
Of humanity, but
A previleged of
The few

It happened
In the past and its
Happening today,
But under a more
Sophisticated ways,
It's called,
"Globalization" and
Tomorrow we call it,
"AIs to be our
New Masters!"

# Participants

How long
To keep praying
Before the world
Sinks under the
Command of the
Seven sin?

Isn't it
Action time with
Rational clarity
And compassion
To yield some
Good results in time

Let's
Open the minds
Let's
Extend the arms
Of friendship

Let's
Get off the
Passive believing
And debating and

Let's
Just roll up the
Sleeves and be worthy
Of our intelligence and
Common sense...

# Sequential

On coming
Closer to my inner
Being, I demanded,
"Who they were"

Silently,
They kept walking
Toward my world

"Stop, please
Tell me why are
You here"

"We're sum
Total of you from
The past"

"What do you mean?"

"Means, we're
Your continuum;
What you've been
Since the beginning..."

"Explain that to me"

They laughed and
Said, "We're all births,
Deaths and rebirths of you;
Ready to absorb you soon..."

# Long
# Walk

Been walking
Many millennia
And the end seems
For every turning
Point of our journey
That we're on

We've been
Ready to leap with
Great anticipation
Toward the ultimate
Meaning of us

And the
Riddle never leaves
The doubtful mind

Is this
Existence either
A magic or just another
Mirage or what?

Damn right,
We've been on the
Trail for a very long
And the journey seems
Stretching to the infinity,
Forever...

# The
# Code

Each
Intelligent being
In the universe is a
Unwritten moral code

That is
The stability force
In this otherwise
Chaotic reality, we're
Trying to know
Bit more

All intelligent
Being who've
Accidentally landed
On the Planet Blue
Too are the
Elegant Unity at
Their very source

Funny,
"Why aren't they
In sync with the basic
Universal essence after all!"

# Legacy

Though
Nothing is certain
And nothing is
Absolute either
Before or after ever

Please leave
A little note behind,
"How you became
While being with us"

Against all
Odds of life,
Still leave a
Petite note behind;
Sharing
Your worth with the
World you were once
For a brief

Don't
Ignore the request
Don't go away without
A word and don't leave
Us in the dark please...

# On
# The Track

After a
Long, let's keep
The flow toward
Our main mission

Yes,
It's pertinent
We understand the
Value of our time
While walking along
The set track

I mean,
Existence is all
About "Point Upward"
Yes, for the Good of
The whole

Let it
Be the forward
Thrust of determination,
Courage and compassion
To win the battle we've
Been in since the beginning...

# Pure
# Freedom

Let
Lovers continue
To dream forever

Let them
Discover the beauty
Of their humanity
At the very core

Let
Lovers wonder
With zillion smiling
Stars in their romantic
State of the mind

Let lovers
All over the world
Come together and
Reverberate the
Hearts of billion
Others every time

Oh yes,
Let lovers be
United to build a
World of rhythms,
Melodies and meaning
Before it's too late...

# Self-will

Human
Shall be the
Full human,
*Sensu strictu*

When
He evolves from
Material bondage
To the pure spiritual
Awareness

Let it be
The rationale to
Steady the world of
Violence, destructions
And deaths

Let's
Discover the
Once lost trail,
Called,
"Enlightenment"

Let's leave
Something of great
Importance to the
Children to follow the
Set trail...

# Crux

If reality
Is the projected
Single cosmic light
Why is it
Leaving darkness
In the intelligent
Minds

If truth
Is the best and
Lasting endurance
Why is it not spilling
Over a tiny bit in the
Will of the intelligent
Beings

Why
So many obsessions
Of the Divine Being
When human got the
Potential to be the
One!

# Moral
# Might

When purity
Of thought and
Action is the habit
Of the living human

He's the
Genuine expression
Of the noble soul, but
Sadly, most of us not
There yet

The journey
Begins when the
Disciplined mind
That rolls the ball

In other
Words, when
Human is willing
To take a bold leap
Forward with the
Mighty moral force...

# Chin-up

Did we
Ever reckon,
"We're the constant
Meditation since the
Birth to death and
Thence to eternity
As ever"

Did we
Ever realize,
"We're the
Wave-makers of
All that is called,
Great Puzzle,
Yet to be untied"

I mean,
We're
The creators,
"What is
Between
The known and
The unknown"

Come and
Let's celebrate our
Beautiful existence
That's a million ton of
All Essence..."

# Solitude

Time
To seek solitude
And be free from
The selfish existence

Let's
Rethink, "How to
Escape these struggles,
Violence's and unfairness"

No, no
Don't run away from
The challenging scene,
But be bold and genius
To change the human
Nature itself

That is
How solitude must
Take us from suffering
To an efflorence bliss...

# Live or
# Die

Only
Nobility of
The inner being
Is the first-hand
Experience to be

Only
Revelation
Valid is, "Sanctum
Of the Moral Self,
Leading to the truth
We've been seeking
Forever, indeed"

Only
The solemn Soul
And Truth are the
Constant
While rest other:
Lives, decays and dies,
Time after time

That seems to be
The ultimate answer
To the quest we've been
On since the beginning...

# Let's
# Celebrate

Folks
Let's
Enjoy every
Celebration no
Matter where
It comes from

Let's just
Forget our troubles
And be the family of
Hope and happiness

Folks
We're here to
Make sense of our
Worthy births;
Why shouldn't we
In harmony together

Let's just
Learn to be friends
And continue to dance
In this beautiful moments
Of this coexistence...

# Difference Makers

Come and
Boomerang the
Passive world with
Some reminders
Today

Let each
Born must stand
To triumph moral
Order over the chaos
And evil forces of
Our time

Let it
Be the sacred
Mission to calm down
The world of constant
Fear and anxiety

Let each
Born to be the
Guardian of harmony
And hope to every
Generation to follow

Let each be
The hero of his
Awakened inner being
All the way to the end...

# What Is

There is
Nothing either
Higher or lower
In the big scheme of
The reality we're in

There is
Nothing either
Sacred or immoral
In the big blueprint
Of the Truth we're
Seeking

It's all
The conceptual
References to hold
The spider-web
With some meaning

After all,
This contextual
Reality must be in order
To keep the train going,
Or else
We shall never make
It to the next station...

# Introspection

Why can't
We come to our
One universal
Common sense

That there
Are no geographic
Man-made claimed
God (or Gods)

Instead,
There is
Only One Eternal
Meaning, yet to be
Known

A meaning
That shall drive
Humanity along a
Right path:
Dignity,
Grace, Harmony
And the Truth,
*All That Is...*

# Free
# To Be

To keep the
Mind calm and
Alert at all time

To keep the
Point of view
Within reason
And openness

Rituals,
Prayers
And worships are
Okay for a while,
But moral act
Be the attention

Being is
Born to be an
Illumined thought and
To be free from the
Imposed beliefs and
Many unnecessary
Pre-requisites...